Help!
These Kids
Are Driving Me
Crazy

Ronald D. Carter

Department of Special Education
University of Wisconsin
Oshkosh, Wisconsin

Research Press
2612 North Mattis Avenue
Champaign, Illinois 61820

15 14 13 12 11 10   81 82 83 84

Copies of this book may be ordered from the publisher
at the address given on the title page.

Printed in the United States of America.

ISBN 0-87822-006-2

Illustrations by Nancy Kingery

Acknowledgments

Thanks goes to my teachers. Among them are my professors, my family, my fellow teachers, and kids. Were it possible to name them one by one, I would happily do so; but, mainly for fear of the risk of embarrassment to my former professors, I will omit the long list.

Contents

Introduction

Dear Colleague:

We have all seen new teachers practically driven out of the classroom by "lively" students. But some teachers aren't.

We also know teachers who get most of their exercise chasing nascent sprinters up and down aisles or ducking erasers from second grade pitchers. But some teachers don't.

Some teachers openly declare that half their time is spent in creating sufficient environmental quietude and attending behavior to allow for some (even a little) teaching. Other classes are calm and quiet.

Still other teachers might just as well lecture to thirty statues for all the good it does to have the attention of students who are scared to death. But not so with all teachers.

So—what do we do?

How do we strike the balance between classroom chaos and prison regimentation?

This book attempts to give teachers some knowledge of workable techniques for humane classroom control, many of which you have known and used for years. It is for all teachers who have ever uttered, with some conviction, "Help! These Kids Are Driving Me Crazy."

Respectfully yours,

Ronald D. Carter, Teacher

1

Living, behaving, and changing

1

Today, right now, let's look at the real "zing" you get out of teaching.

Why do you like it? Because you're a good teacher!

Why is it you're a good teacher and some people aren't?

The best place to look is at YOU, in your classroom. What do you do in your classroom that's better? It's pleasant there; it's a productive place, too.

But what is it that you DO that makes it so? Don't tell me that you're the type of person who simply lives life and loves it. Because it really doesn't tell me what I can DO to be a good teacher, too. Tell me what YOU DO!

What you do

YOU, of all people, recognize that worlds aren't made in a day. They're put together piece by piece. It takes care, thought, love, lots of guts, and a plan.

How about a kid's self-esteem? It's just like those worlds that aren't made in a day. You work hard — day after day — putting pieces together.

You help (prompt) him when he's wrong; you support him when he's right; you tell his buddies how great he's doing.

But, hey—our cart's almost before our horse.

"The 'stuff' of self-esteem"

What is it you're "tinkering" with when you're building that self-esteem? What are your building blocks, TEACHER?

Your blocks, my friend, are simply the things you get Johnnie to **do.**

> He **behaves.**
> He **acts.**
> He **does.**

Every single move Johnnie makes is the "stuff" of self-esteem.

> It's **behavior.**

Certainly, it's behavior. Nothing more, nothing less—it's pure old, down-to-earth behavior.

4

And you have
1. the skill,
2. the training, and
3. the responsibility
to guide that behavior.

But a behavior is...

This all sounds marvelous but looking more closely at what you do is crucial, HERE!

You don't deal with big philosophical constructs in the middle of reading class.

I see you asking some of these questions:
1. Is Gretel following the place?
2. How about Hermione? Is she saying the "a" sound correctly in new words?
3. Are both of Harvey's feet where they belong?
4. Did Martin tell us the story *correctly* in his own words?

Observables: Behaviors

You seem to be concerned with each little tiny event—each observable thing the kid does.

So, what most people loosely call a kid's behavior, then, is made up of a whole bunch of little bitty behaviors—all readily discernible (seeable) in the here and now. Right?

Really, then, a behavior is **anything** a person **does.**

> . . . And **that's** what **you** work with.

You try to improve Hermione's reading behavior. At the same time, you're improving Harvey's behavior with feet. You're grappling with everything that each kid does.

> . . . every discernible event!

For example...

When Hermione learns the "a" sound and Harvey learns where to keep his feet, the job's not over, of course. But, in both cases, you've taught a behavior that, when properly placed in its niche, leads to reading, in one case, and being a good neighbor, in the other.

Clearly, you've methodically taught a part of a bigger behavior.

But, how do you know when you've taught it? You can see the kids doing the little behaviors (the tiny building blocks) that you've taught them.

Hermione says "a" correctly.
Harvey keeps his feet in place.

Now, you go on to the next behavior in those *awesome things* called **reading** or **being a good neighbor**?

Through all this you're making an assumption. What is it you're assuming as you move step by step in the teaching-learning process?

It seems that you're saying:
Hermione's behavior is learned. Harvey's behavior is learned.

And—
You're teaching it!

Since we seem to see eye to eye, how about letting me speak for you. . .
It may help you recognize many good things you do in your classroom, and besides talking for both of us really turns me on.

To summarize

Behavior is taught by someone.
So, two people are involved—a *learner* and *teacher.*

The things we do (our behaviors) have been brought about by the behaviors of someone else. In essence, we can say that someone *taught* us or *trained* us to behave as we do.

Teachers teach or train their students' behaviors.

Parents teach or train their children's behaviors.

In fact, most of us also recognize that children teach and train *us*—their teachers and parents.

Actually, in all life situations, we effect the behaviors of others and they, in turn, effect our behaviors.

How about that for equality!

Some special things to remember

Well, the first thing is to avoid hoping that regardless of what we do—be it right or wrong—that by some magic inherent in the child, he will "blossom" into a "good grown-up."

Being a good teacher or being a good parent are not instinctive. Then, how in heaven's name can we rationalize our hoping that "being a good kid," "being a bright boy," or "being a nice guy" is instinctive for a child?

Somewhere, sometime, teachers have to be taught *how* to be *good teachers.*

Likewise, kids have to be taught *how* to be *good kids.*

So, the second thing we must do is to realize that to be a *good teacher,* or to be a *good kid,* the desired behavior *must* be taught.

The third thing we should realize is that the foregoing is in no way designed to imply that kids, teachers, or parents don't eventually develop the skill of figuring things out for themselves.

Indeed, they do!

However, being a *good anything* in reasonable time demands *good training.*

In order to just do a good job of teaching kids in a natural manner we have to be taught—initially. Having done it a few times in a stiff and unnatural way, it *slowly* becomes second nature.

In other words, we graduate to the level of functioning where we can figure things out for ourselves . . . but graduation suggests that we've been taught some basics along the way.

A good example of this might be the job interview. Before we can really know what is expected in an interview situation, we have to have had at least one job interview. Having lived through one, we're able to handle similar situations in the future. We are able to apply this old knowledge to the new situation.

The skill of applying old knowledge is the hitch . . . very difficult to learn . . . even for us adults.

Changing

Fortunately, behavior **can be changed.** Goodness knows our kids learn things we don't like them to learn. But on the other hand, they learn lots of good things, too.

It probably makes good sense to say that . . .

If children learn their behaviors from other people, we can simply change what we teach them.

If we change what we teach them, there should be a change in our learner's behavior. Isn't that sensible?

On the other hand, we can clarify what we're teaching . . . and sometimes find that we do not have to change what we are teaching. Rather, we simply have to make clear exactly what we are attempting to teach.

In other words, it is important not to cloud the issue when we are teaching a behavior.

For example, most teachers recognize the absurdity and the difficulty involved if they were to try to teach a child (1) reading comprehension, (2) penmanship, (3) word recognition, and (4) spelling accuracy all at the same time in a single lesson.

(But sometimes we teachers try it anyway.)

There's still hope

Teachers can improve their practices in teaching or training youngsters.

Teachers are concerned with trying to help children grow up to be successful adults.

In fact, most adults are in the business of teaching children. They are trying to establish desirable behavior in the child.

Once the desired behavior shows up in the child, the next step is to maintain it.

That's what the goals of teaching are all about. We want to maintain good performance.

Strengthening desirable behaviors

2

This manual describes what is referred to as principles of behavior modification for the classroom teacher.

Teachers and parents (and bosses at work, for that matter) generally ask four important questions:

How can I get him **to do that?**

Now that he **does that,** how can I keep **that** going?

How can I get him **not to do that?** Now that he **doesn't do that,** how can I keep **that** going?

These two groups of questions demonstrate the two major ideas of this manual and the two major parts of behavior modification.

Behavior can be strengthened! And by the same token, **behavior can be weakened!** (But we'll get to that later.)

Behavior can be increased or decreased in its frequency of occurrence. Frequency is our yardstick for measuring whether the behavior is stronger or weaker.

When we want to influence the behavior of a student, we say either . . .

- that we want him to do something, or
- that we want him to not do something

. . . each time the opportunity comes around.

In the case of *desirable behaviors,* we say "How do I get it? How do I keep it?"

In the case of *undesirable behaviors,* we say "How do I get rid of it? How do I keep rid of it?"

Looking at our own lives we discover that for us the *results* of our behavior are the things that determine whether we engage in an activity again. The same is true for kids.

The **key word** is **consequences!**

Consequences are what mold behavior

Parents and teachers mold behavior simply by manipulating the consequences of behavior.

To manipulate consequences is not harmful, immoral, or unethical. In fact, we do it already. Each of us can recall hundreds of times that we've told someone "thanks" for doing something nice for us. Is that manipulating consequences?

Sure it is.

Let's analyze the events:

BEHAVIOR ⟶ CONSEQUENCE

10:03 a.m.   10:04 a.m.

A nice deed occurs.   You say "thanks."

In this example, someone did something and your "thanks" was the *result* or the *consequence*. He'll probably do nice things for you again. He probably won't for the guy who doesn't say "thanks."

So, the fellow's behavior is manipulated by the *results* it yields him.

Similarly, wives cook breakfast for crabby husbands—when the consequences are right. If Hubby doesn't come through with proper consequences, however, breakfast probably stops or at least gets worse. On the other hand, if Hubby remembers anniversaries, birthdays, and Mother's Day, breakfast probably continues or maybe even gets better.

Finally, if employees go to work, they are paid. If they don't go, pay stops.

If we **change the consequence,**
we **change the behavior.**

So, to a large extent, we are forced to recognize that adult (and child) behaviors are controlled by their *consequences*. It looks like this:

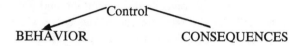

BEHAVIOR   CONSEQUENCES

Now, let's go a little further by considering this:

BEHAVIOR   CONSEQUENCE

Come to work→(and then)→ you get *paid*.

But, notice that if the consequence is changed your *behavior* will be changed.

BEHAVIOR   CONSEQUENCE

Come to work→(and then)→ you *don't* get paid.

You *don't* come to work→(and then)→

_____.

you fill in the rest.

The point is that much of what we do in the "here and now" is related to what will happen soon afterwards.

16

Giver and receiver of consequences

Each of us has probably already figured out that sometimes we're the giver and sometimes we're the receiver.

Simply stated:

1. Sometimes we do a behavior and wait for the consequences from the boss, the teacher, or Mommy or Daddy.

2. Sometimes others do the behavior and wait for our consequences such as "Thank you," "What a thoughtful thing to do," "Here's your pay check."

Yes, to some extent, our behaviors are controlled by other people. But don't despair. We control their behavior, too.

It's nothing more than a give and take situation. We scratch each other's backs. In fact, it's not possible to avoid this type of interaction. Not even if we try.

Reinforcers

It is accepted by most authorities that we use the term *reinforcer* to describe pay checks, "thanks," and cards on Mother's Day.

These things happen to us as a result of nice things we've done in the past. Yes, a consequence for our behavior.

In fact, if we look back over the years, the money, the cards, or the kind words are the things that keep us going—at least to some extent.

We continue fixing breakfast and going to work . . . **but** just think what we'd really do if everyone stopped reinforcing us. We'd probably stop doing many of the things we do now.

Stopping reinforcement wouldn't be awful; it wouldn't be nasty; it wouldn't be immoral. We'd probably just do something else instead, like go fishing, read a good book, listen to the radio, or simply rest for a change. We'd engage in some behavior that *has an immediate reinforcer* (pay-off) built into it for us.

For example, some people read a lot just because they like to read. It's reinforcing in and of itself. Some ladies sew simply because they like to sew. We might say that they are able to reward themselves.

You've been waiting for this...

Alas, people are not completely controlled by the consequences that *others* provide—only mostly. Otherwise, many people would spend more time on their hobbies than they do on their jobs.

But, we are bound to an arrangement (WORK = $$$$) that requires our devoting a large segment of each day to working for reinforcers that other people give out.

18

Kinds of reinforcers

Roughly, there are three types of reinforcers that influence our behavior:

OTHERS-CONTROLLED

1. Tangibles ($$$$, candy)
2. Non-tangibles (praise, smiles)

SELF-CONTROLLED

3. Non-tangibles (sewing, reading)

The higher the number, the more the person is operating towards maturity. However, we all operate at all levels in our everyday lives.

We teachers think that all kids should love to learn in school—simply because it can be fun and exciting. But, we both know that to do that phonics worksheet for the fun of learning requires a fairly high level of maturity on the part of *some* kids. There are, nevertheless, some other kids who do it eagerly.

Let's analyze these possibilities. . .

1. The child could do his school work because we give him goodies or some kind of tangible reward.

2. The child could do his school work because we praise him for doing it.

3. The child could do his school work for the joy of learning.

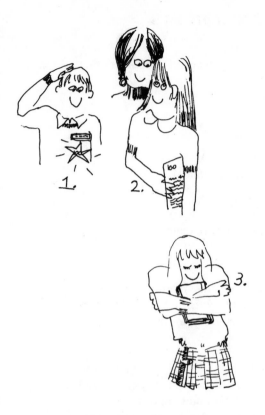

If our student simply can't function on "the joy of learning" level of pay-off, it is conceivable that praise or even a piece of dry cereal might be the way to get this kid on the ball at first.

Each time it occurs, we pay off for good performance . . . with different things for different kids.

Later, when the child is performing fairly well, we begin weaning him from the goodies and bringing on the praise. Later still, we wean out the praise (somewhat) and he's suddenly working "under his own steam," so to speak.

Labeling our ideas

For our purposes:

Level 1 reinforcers have no special name except **tangible rewards.**

Level 2 is generally called **social reinforcement.**

Level 3 is called **self-reinforcement.**

More specifically, social reinforcement can be a teacher's smile, parental attention (a listening ear), a pat on the back, or a "Yes, that's right." It's simply those nice little things we do for people to let them know we care—we appreciate what they just did that preceded our delivery of the reinforcer.

At Level 3 (self-reinforcement), reinforcers come from within the person himself. They are non-tangible. Each of us likes to engage in certain behaviors just because they are fun. Such things as reading, sex, eating, and walking in the woods alone are examples of Level 3 reinforcers.

Although not really this clear-cut, we might say that in terms of our jobs we use tangible kinds of pay-offs. On the patio with friends we use social reinforcers. In the den, when we're all alone, we are functioning on self-reinforcers.

Remember, though, *behavior is learned.* Someone had to teach us. None of us "knew" instinctively which levels to use, at what times, and in what settings. We all had to be taught.

Furthermore, it took time and practice to get there—to have our lives nicely and neatly compartmentalized as we have them now.

Kids simply haven't "arrived yet." They need to rely on *us* to teach them.

Now comes the real punch

Kids can also be trained to graduate from level to level to level of reinforcement. Consider for a moment the "older kid"—believe it or not—who does his school work just because he likes it. These kids have learned to get their thrills from things other than just tangible reinforcers. The enjoyment of their school work is rewarding solely on its own.

Strange?

Perhaps.

But, it's more common than some people think.

When we start to train our child, we may have to "pay off" for good work in terms of tangibles for some defiant kids. Later on, after they are hooked, we can help them to derive benefit from the work itself.

Thus far, we have discussed how behavior is subject to what happens next. In other words, behavioral control is associated with its consequences.

Nailing down a definition

By this time, you may have partially discovered the scientific definition of a reinforcer or "pay-off."

**A reinforcer is
(Nothing more than)
Anything that causes
A behavior to recur
More frequently**

Kinds of consequences

Things other than just reinforcers can happen to us when we do something.

Actually, there are three types of consequences:

1. reinforcers,
2. punishers, and
3. blahs (neutral events).

Reinforcers

As we've seen, reinforcers have a clear-cut effect on behavior. They increase the behavior's frequency. Reinforcers cause a behavior to happen more often when the opportunity for it occurs. We might say that we've strengthened the behavior.

To be quite formal, we have increased the probability with which the desired behavior will occur, given the appropriate conditions for performing that behavior.

Obviously, kids don't walk around saying "thanks." They say it only when the conditions are right, for example, when you give them candy. If you want them to learn to say "thanks" for the candy, you'd probably want to praise them at age two when they remember to say it. By the time they're four, the youngsters will probably remember to say "thanks" more readily.

So, once again, we return to the general principle of "plan for the future." Expecting good behavior to occur instinctively is . . . well . . . er . . . stupid. Let's face it, we have to train it.

Look beyond the "here and now" and arrange the consequences so you can reinforce only the behavior you desire. We have to do this for the child's own good and for our sanity.

Punishers

Punishers are also a possible consequence of behavior.

For example, if you say "That's a sharp tie," and I say (with a sneer), "Oh, you always say that," you'll probably tell me to get lost or something even more spicy.

In this case, I've given you a *punisher* as a consequence of what you said to me. You'll probably conclude, and reasonably so, that I'm a heel, and that I am no longer deserving of such kind comments in the future.

I've decreased the frequency of your "kind commenting behavior." From now on, you'll throw your bouquets in other directions. Or you might simply keep quiet from now on.

Punishers are a useful consequence which we can use to decrease behavior. However, the devastating effects of punishers are such that we *must use them sparingly*. We'll discuss punishment in more detail later.

Blahs

Finally, another kind of consequence that we apply to behavior is the "blah" or neutral consequence. It neither reinforces (increases) nor punishes (decreases) the preceding behavior. It *has no impact at all*. It just happens.

For example, after seeing a show on TV that turned you on, you might turn to a friend and say, "Wasn't that a great show!" He responds, "You know, I enjoy good TV shows."

In this example, your friend was evasive. He neither reinforced nor punished your comment.

24

We might say he "blahed it." He said something that failed to indicate either his degree of or his lack of agreement with you. You clearly indicated that you wanted an opinion. And he simply said that he liked good TV shows. Who knows what that means with respect to *your* question!

Given only the above information, it's impossible to predict what you might do next. Some people would pursue the issue (because they've been reinforced for pursuing issues).

Others, however, might drop that topic because they've been taught that perseverance in these situations doesn't pay off.

Clearly, we'd have to know more about you and how you've been reared to predict with good odds what you might do next.

Three rules for tools

1. A *reinforcer* gives us a *charge to our battery* . . ."I'll do that again, if that's what I get."

2. A *punisher turns us off* . . . "I'll never do that again, if you're going to act that way about it."

3. A *blah,* the *neutral* event, simply is . . . "water off a duck's back."

It just happens. It has no influence on our behavior.

Rationalizing consequences

For some strange reason, it is unnecessary to describe **in detail** to the child the reasons why we reinforce him for his behavior. (The point here is that the verbal description is nothing more than an extra, added attraction—the pat on the head is enough.)

This point is most easily demonstrated by the fact that performers have trained circus animals for years to do what is expected. And animals still don't understand a word of English. How could this training possibly happen?

Our rational powers tell us that animal trainers don't really have "special communication skills." Although we might not think so sometimes, these trainers are just like you and me.

But . . .

The art of training a child, an adult (or even a chimpanzee) is to deliver that almighty reinforcer. As soon as the desired behavior occurs, pay off!

Don't wait; don't save up. Goodness knows, too few of us adults have savings accounts anyway . . . inflation and all that.

Rules for getting a desired behavior

Immediate reinforcement of the desired behavior is the key to strengthening or increasing behavior. The behavior will recur because it was somehow "nice" for the learner.

26

Withholding or delaying our pay-off simply works against us. Literally, if we stop reinforcing a behavior, it will stop happening. The reasons are clear; pleasing consequences have been removed.

When we delay reinforcement, the amount of change or improvement will be proportionally delayed.

Thus, the sooner we pay off for the desired behavior *only,* the sooner we'll reap the benefits of our work. Saving up or delaying reinforcement slows down the whole training process.

Do you already know the rule?

Rule 1. Reinforce immediately.

Rule 1 Reinforce immediately

Selecting appropriate reinforcers

Another consideration that teachers must face is "What can I use as a reinforcer?"

This question presents a very real problem for us all. Although there is a clear-cut answer, it does not reduce the burden for the teacher.

The answer, plain and simple, is:
Look at the child's behavior.

By this it is meant that people vary widely in the things they like. Some of us enjoy rhubarb, others like steak.

As a result, it is necessary that we individualize or tailor the reinforcers to fit the child. Some kids like ice cream, some like candy. Still others like dry cereal and others like adult attention.

The suggestion, then, is to determine what turns your kid(s) on. Then, *use it!* Use those things to reward desirable behaviors. Withhold them when desired behaviors are not present.

Up against the wall???

Teachers, nevertheless, sometimes wind up pinned in a little. They say, "I've tried everything and there's nothing he'll work for."

That's just not true.

There's *something* that each of us likes. It's harder to find out about some people's preferences than it is with others. There's no doubt about that.

An attempt to resolve this dilemma (and it's met with much success so far) has been to ask the youngster, "What would you like to work for?"

Chances are, he'll tell you.

And this is where the problem begins . . .

Problems

One teacher says, "Yes, but he should already be doing that in this grade."

Another teacher may consider that hot rod magazines are a waste of time.

Principals may say " . . . and she's not teaching a thing to that class . . . " if the youngsters have five minutes to "goof off" at the end of the period.

> AND THIS IS WHERE THE PROBLEM
> ENDS . . . REALLY!

Teachers, principals, and parents must be willing to give an inch RIGHT NOW in order to gain a mile IN THE LONG RUN!

Kids' pay-offs

No doubt many of the things valued by teenagers or nursery school kiddies are silly to us grown-ups.

For example "Who wants to read those silly romance magazines?"

"No, honey, you don't need to watch this commercial; you can already sing it forwards and backwards anyway. Come on to bed."

We adults often push *our own values on kids*. We're interested in stressing the merits of good citizenship, scholarship, patriotism, strong moral ethics, and good personal hygiene, to name only a few of the more important things in life.

**We ignore those things
That "turn on" the kids
And can be used as
The kids' reinforcers**

The fact of the matter is that ninety seconds of extra recess time may not be particularly groovy to you teacher, but it is for thirty-five second-graders in your class.

This argument for the younger generation is not an effort to make you or any adult a push-over or easy game. Rather, it is an attempt to make the obvious reinforcers work for you.

An example...

Sue seldom picks up her clothes.

Sue wants the freedom to stay out until 11:00 on Saturdays rather than just 10:00.

One way to handle this issue is to require a "picked-up room" everyday for one week.

Naturally, if the behavior (picking up for a week) occurs, you'll want to reinforce it on Saturday with an extra hour.

In more detail, so she can be sure she's really making progress (and so you can be sure too), try this:

Give her ten points per day and charge her sixty points for one additional hour—to be used only on Saturday nights.

Make your goals and
The child's goals meet
On a common ground

"You do what I want. Then, you can do what you want."

The above solution to a management problem is nothing more than the traditional contract. "You pay me $5, then I'll give you the goods."

The fact that you don't really think Sue needs that extra hour on Saturday night is not the issue. Nor is the fact that the salesman might know that you don't need the merchandise that you're buying.

The fact is:

What *Sue* values is important and desirable to her. She thinks she needs that hour.

What *you* value is important and desirable to you. You think you need the merchandise.

The extra (perhaps not needed) hour certainly won't cause a family crisis. Further, selling you an extra (perhaps not needed) bracelet or pair of cuff links won't cause the salesman any great anxiety—even if he does know you need the money for groceries.

In both cases, the receiver made his purchase. He must take what he bargained for.

31

Now look what was gained . . .

SUE:

1. You got a cleaned up room for a week.
2. Sue got her precious hour.

YOU:

1. The salesman got his $5.
2. You got your extra jewelry.

The significance of this whole discussion centers around the *learner*. What is it that he'll work for? Either watch him or ask him outright. You'll be surprised at the response you'll get.

How teachers can handle pay-offs: A recipe

One way that teachers have been able to handle the problem of individualizing reinforcers in a group of thirty or more youngsters is to develop a **class menu.**

1. Students supply the list of things they want to earn.

2. By a hand vote, they indicate what they generally like most, next most, and so on.

3. The teacher simply assigns a high point value to the most desired items and fewer points as the items decrease in desirability.

Then, through earning points, the youngsters have something that they like that they can work for.

4. Points are awarded for *good work*.

5. And, subsequently, purchasing power bespeaks its own merit.

Here's a sample menu . . .

DAILY CLASS MENU

Reinforcers	Price
Extra recess — 5 minutes	1000 points
Extra recess — 3 minutes	950 points
Wash boards	925 points
Pass out books	850 points
Hall monitor	800 points
Free time — 10 minutes	750 points
Free time — 5 minutes	725 points
Free time — 2 minutes	715 points
Extra recess — 1 minute	700 points
Empty trash for teacher	650 points
Answer door	500 points
Lead the flag salute	400 points
Count for milk break	350 points
Library time — 10 minutes	250 points
Library time — 5 minutes	200 points
Rest — 5 minutes	150 points

Recapping

We have discussed both

1. the importance of being quick on the trigger with reinforcers, and

2. the importance of tailoring reinforcers to what the child wants.

And, we have worked up to another rule.

Rule 2. Tailor reinforcers to pupil preferences.

Rule 2: Tailor reinforcers to pupil preferences

Regular and immediate reinforcement

Now we have realized that what we "think" *should be* reinforcing is of no earthly use. The important thing is to discover *what it is* that's reinforcing from the youngster's point of view.

Another factor that determines our success with kids is *our behavior*.

If we pay off for awhile and then stop suddenly, kids say we "copped out."

If we pay off one day, not on another, and then pay off again on still another day, we've still created a "generation gap." In so doing we've clearly demonstrated that

Adults are indeed the enemy!

We have then given concrete evidence that adults are *unreliable* or at best, they are *inconsistent*. They don't really mean what they say.

The solution to this problem is at least partially obvious to us all. If we're going to reinforce a particular behavior, we must stick to our guns. We must reinforce the desired behavior *immediately* and *regularly*.

The point of this whole discussion is that we teachers and parents must set up *predictable reinforcers* for kids. If we want consistently good performance from the child, our behavior must also be consistent.

Have you guessed the next rule?

Rule 3. Don't ignore a good performance.

Catch kids being good

If we adults allow a desirable behavior to sneak by unreinforced, we've goofed. We lose an opportunity to influence that behavior.

don't ignore a good performance

In essence, adults must learn to be good detectives.

Some teachers are probably already saying, "I can't possibly be everywhere at once." Certainly not. You can't be teaching phonics or biology and simultaneously reinforcing other students' behaviors out in the gym for good cooperative play.

Rather, the issue is:

Anytime you are around when cooperative play occurs, then *sound off about it*.

Deliver your reinforcer (1) right after the behavior happens (2) in your presence.

Pointers about reinforcing

In general, we have to be around when it happens, if we're trying to change *social behaviors* (such as being friendly, saying "please" and "thank you," and "excuse me"). It's not really too safe to take other people's word about whether or not "it" has occurred. You'd best be there yourself and know for sure.

Yes, you're right. **Social behaviors,** like **social reinforcers,** are not tangible.

For the more tangible things in life such as (1) getting her teeth brushed, (2) putting gas in the car after each Saturday night, (3) doing the dishes, (4) doing the homework, and (5) putting his shoes on the correct feet, we may not have to always be around to establish that "it" has happened.

However, when in question, if the desired behavior has occurred, either be there or look for concrete evidence.

So, tell me the next rule.

Rule 4. If you plan to reinforce a behavior when it occurs, then BE SURE IT OCCURS, i.e., be sneaky and catch 'em being good.

One last pointer

To modify a child's behavior, we must also *examine our own behavior*.

We provide the conditions for kids to learn behavior.

By this it is meant that we tell the kid "Hey, now's the time to say 'thank you'" or "Now, get out your reading books."

This'll make it a little clearer:

It would be a bit bizarre should three-year-old Magda hop out of bed at midnight to put on her panties "frontwards." The time to do **that** is (1) in the morning when she gets up, or (2) when Mommie says to do it.

Clearly, Magda probably won't pull her midnight caper too many times, if it goes **unreinforced.** In other words, she'll soon learn **when** (under what conditions) putting on her panties is **reinforced.**

Another slant on this idea might be:

$$\text{REINFORCER} = \frac{\overset{1}{\text{Something}}\ \overset{2}{\text{that causes a behavior to recur,}}}{\underset{\textit{when} \text{ you want it to recur.}}{\overset{3}{}}}$$

In our definition . . .

The #1 corresponds to our "pay-off" (the consequences). The #2 corresponds to the child's behavior (that you want). The #3 corresponds to the conditions under which the behavior is supposed to occur.

. . . back to Magda . . .

So if Magda doesn't quite know when it's time to do her special clothing thing,

For goodness sake tell her!

Each of us knows how useful it is to have **hints,**
clues, and **cues.**

One way that some teachers have used this
method wisely is to develop a list of **"classroom**
hints."

For example...

We raise our hands to talk.
We walk in the halls.
We write *only* on our papers.
We keep feet quiet in class.

Notice that in each case this teacher has given
some useful clues to her class. She specifies
what is expected and *when* to do it.

Guessed the final rule?

Rule 5. Clearly specify WHEN (under what
conditions) a behavior is desired.

In summary

We can take a sequence of events and identify
the important components:

Event 1	**Event 2**	**Event 3**
Preferred	Desired	Consequences
Circumstances	Behavior	

When my grass gets tall, **you** cut it, and I'll pay you $2.

Going a little further...

Adults control Events 1 and 3. (We determine *when* we want something to happen. We also are the ones who deliver the pay-off.)

Kids control or do Event 2.

The classroom implications of this summary are that (1) to get kids to read (Event 2), a teacher must have appropriate materials (Event 1), before she can reinforce (Event 3) the desired behavior; and (2) to get kids to stop hitting their playmates (Event 2), a teacher should describe *when* exactly (Event 1) hitting can and can't occur, before the teacher can reinforce (Event 3) the absence of hitting behavior.

Clearly specify _when_ behavior is desired

Weakening undesirable behaviors 3

We have already established that behavior can be either *strengthened* or *weakened*.

We usually try to strengthen desirable behaviors and we try to weaken undesirable behaviors.

This chapter is devoted to the "HOW TO" for getting rid of undesirable behaviors.

As before, the **key word** is **consequences!**

Consider for a moment, the consequences we as teachers and parents usually use to weaken behavior.

Sometimes we take away Mary's privileges.

Sometimes we tell Jake how naughty he is.

Finally, we may "blast" Fred when he acts stupid.

Obviously, we're trying to teach each of these kids not to engage in certain undesired behaviors.

These are some of the common ways that we teachers and parents go about controlling our kids, and all these ways fall into the class of techniques called *punishment.*

Does *punishment* get the lasting results we want?

Let's take an example. We'll drop in on a family watching TV . . .

A problem lurks. Burt is hitting his sister, Mildred. For some reason, he can't seem to keep his hands off her. Mildred is ready to throw a raging fit. Dad is watching TV and reading the newspaper. Mom is washing dishes. This is what has happened over the past ten minutes:

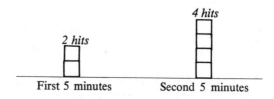

At the end of the first ten minutes, Dad decides to nip the situation in the bud . . .
"Burt, STOP THAT NOW! I'll whack you, if you keep it up."
This is what happens . . .

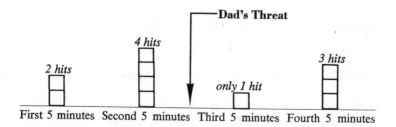

Burt's behavior is immediately affected by Dad's threat.

However, hitting isn't quite wiped out. Slowly, Burt starts up again. Look back at the picture.

At this point, Dad decides to go for a beer and whacks Burt on his way to the kitchen. Burt was just getting ready to do it again.

And this is what happens . . .

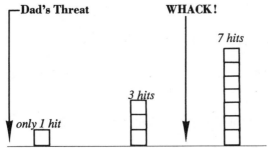

As soon as Dad is out of sight, Burt really lets go. He hits Mildred many more times, and she begins to cry.

Dad suddenly looks through the door and a hush falls over the room.

Without going into further detail, it is clear that we've set up a beautiful game of cat 'n' mouse. Probably, if this vicious circle continues, all three family members are going to collapse in bed—exhausted—maybe even an hour or so before their regular bedtimes.

Surely there's an alternative solution to this melo-drama.

There is.

But, just a minute.

First...

Dad's really not a bad guy. Neither is Burt. They just weren't wearing their "thinking caps," as we say in kindergarten.

Stop and think. How **do** people learn to show desirable behaviors?

Yes. They get **reinforced** for them.

Obviously, Dad wanted a desirable behavior; he wanted Burt to stop hitting.

Dad should pay off when Burt's *not* hitting.

**Being punished
For undesirable behavior
Couldn't possibly
(In a million years)
Teach the desired behavior.**

Punishment, alone, doesn't work.

Yet, most teachers and most parents use a great deal more punishment than reinforcement in training kids.

We *seem* to spend most of our time with our children punishing the naughty things they do, because they *seem* to be doing these naughty things most of the time.

Because we're busy or because we honestly don't know the options available to us, we don't think of any other way to get rid of these naughty behaviors.

46

In fact, we find very few desirable behaviors in our kids to reinforce.

Did I hear you say, "Okay . . . so, what do I do now?"

I hope I did.

Punishment alone doesn't work

Alternatives to punishment

One way to avoid the use of punishment is to supply a **hint** for an *acceptable substitute behavior*.

For example, "Jan, I don't like for you to eat cookies in the living room. You may eat your cookies if you'll go into the kitchen."

In this example, you've specified

1. the conditions (in the kitchen),
2. the behavior (leaving the living room), and
3. the reinforcer (permission to continue eating cookies).

Whew! And not once did anyone have to be unpleasant.

A spin-off of this same idea is to be sure (if you can) that the behavior you recommend is *incompatible* with the "naughty behavior."

For example, kids can't run around the classroom and erase the chalkboard at the same time.

Another alternative

Some of us may be pleased with the above suggestion. The problem, however, is:

"Sometimes I can't think of an *acceptable substitute behavior*. By 2:00 I'm too tired and I want to relax. I'd almost rather let it go, if the behavior's not too bad."

48

Teacher, you're in luck.

Ignoring that "no-no" is the best thing you can do.

Ironically, a large amount of the "little nasties" that kids do are simply *honest attempts* to get someone's (anyone's) attention.

By *ignoring* the *little* "no-no's," we remove the consequences that the kid wants.

If we *ignore* (remove the reinforcer) long enough, the behavior will be weakened or decreased.

The thrill is gone. He no longer gets the "zing" he used to get when he interrupted class discussions.

The first time he goes for 12-15 minutes, without interrupting, say,

"Edgar, I'm proud. You haven't disturbed us lately" and then, you're also reinforcing an **acceptable substitute behavior.**

There are two issues hidden in this discussion:

1. Teachers probably need to stop to consider whether each undesirable behavior is really worth "blasting off" about.

Research shows that ignoring undesirable behavior works.

The power of ignoring is remarkable.

2. Generally, it is helpful to reinforce the behavior you want along with ignoring the one you don't want. Working from both ends of the situation should get faster results.

49

𝒜 warning

Ignoring is very effective, but it's nice to know what to expect when you are using it.

Research in hundreds of real-life situations has shown that you'll usually get *"a little spurt"* in the frequency of the "undesirable behavior" at first. Then, it will die down.

For example...

Up until now, you've always said, "Sara, stop that!" when she taps her pencil.

If you start to ignore it, pencil tapping may slightly increase, and then it will drop off *gradually*.

A picture may help . . .

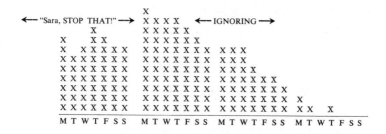

```
                          X
←—"Sara, STOP THAT!"—→   X X X X    ←— IGNORING —→
              X           X X X X X
      X       X X         X X X X X X
      X   X X X X X        X X X X X X X   X X X
   X X X X X X X          X X X X X X X   X X X
   X X X X X X X          X X X X X X X   X X X X
   X X X X X X X          X X X X X X X   X X X X X X
   X X X X X X X          X X X X X X X   X X X X X X X
   X X X X X X X          X X X X X X X   X X X X X X X   X
   X X X X X X X          X X X X X X X   X X X X X X X   X X   X
   M T W T F S S         M T W T F S S   M T W T F S S   M T W T F S S
```

You've probably noticed that even after three weeks of ignoring, pencil tapping still occurs. Perhaps THIS is when you want to start reinforcing COMPLETE failure to tap her pencil.

If it doesn't disappear, but still happens about once a month or so, I guess all we can say is "Well, nobody's perfect." At least 95% of her day is no longer devoted to her pencil — more like only .1% of a month.

A second warning

Ignoring is great. It can work real wonders for teacher, parent, and child.

But . . .

if you use ignoring, be certain the "no-no" doesn't endanger

1. the child himself, or
2. other people.

Then, move onward and upward—full steam ahead with ignoring.

Limitations of punishment

We showed earlier that punishment can get results.

Nagging can decrease a behavior.

The problem is that *the results are short-lived.*

Remember how hitting increased as soon as Dad went for a beer?

Teachers want PERMANENT RESULTS.

You already know your two best weapons:

1. ignoring and
2. providing an acceptable substitute.

Beyond its apparent uselessness, we find that punishment also *creates* problems.

Consequences of punishment

If we punish with regularity, the child associates *us* with the punishment and may act accordingly.

He may try to avoid our class. He may get lost on the way home or think of excuses not to come or dawdle in the previous class or forget to come straight home. He may avoid my presence because the "atmosphere" I create is no longer reinforcing.

These behaviors are called *avoidance reactions*.

Similarly, he may try to escape when we're around. If *I* come into the room, Gomer leaves. As soon as attendance is checked at school, Gus skips school or hides in the restroom.

These behaviors are called *escape reactions*.

Still another reaction may be for the youngster to show great fear or anxiety when we're around. When *I* ask him a question, *Buzz clams up;* he's a chatterbox with everyone else. When *I* walk past Frieda's desk, *she literally shakes,* but she's okay in "what's her name's" class.

These behaviors are called *anxiety reactions*.

In the final analysis, we must recognize that mild punishment leads to only mild reactions. But more severe measures (harsh scoldings, a *real* spanking, etc.) can have effects that are more devastating than the behavior that the kid was involved in, in the first place.

These situations seem almost impossible to reverse.

So, always use punishers with great caution.

Hints, tricks of the trade, and details

4

Hints

Shaping

Sometimes kids can do lots of nice things, but they can't do something that we want them to do.

For example, you might know a seven-year-old who still can't tie her shoes—and she's in the second grade.

One way to cope with this problem is through use of the techniques in the earlier chapters.

Shaping simply involves reinforcing desirable behaviors under the right conditions with one main difference . . .

Shaping is used to teach *complex behaviors.*

To shape a complex behavior, like shoe-tying, we *break it down* into its component parts.

Shoe-tying behavior involves about seven different operations.

Thus, the simplest way to get shoe-tying behavior is to reinforce each of these separate operations.

After they are each mastered, then, reinforce completing operations 1 and 2 as a unit. Then, reinforce 1, 2, and 3 as a unit. Keep expanding the unit to be reinforced until it includes all seven components.

Over a reasonably brief period of time, the seven *separate* steps will become "welded" together as a single unit—shoe-tying behavior.

And, your goal is reached!

The only caution is this...

If you've been reinforcing steps 1, 2, and 3 *as a unit, never* give in and reinforce doing *only* steps 1 and 2 as a unit. You've caused the child to graduate beyond that by this time.

Thus, *never* allow the child to take a backwards step.

Behavior maintenance

Once you've got the behavior you want, *never* pay off for anything less — regardless of the begging or pleading. Stick to your guns. Once you've achieved top performance, always demand it in the future.

Timing and reinforcers

You've already learned two rules for *when* to reinforce:

1. Reinforce immediately, and
2. Reinforce regularly.

BUT . . .

Another aspect of timing is related to *our* time schedules. Sometimes (regardless of why) we aren't able to continue to pay off regularly once we've got the desired behavior.

Maybe there's another child in your class who is also needing a lot of individualized attention too.

As a matter of fact, once we've reached our goal (e.g., doing two whole rows of problems) we can "slack up."

By this is meant, instead of reinforcing *every time* the behavior occurs, we can simply increase the amount of work required for each reinforcer.

For example, Warner must do three lines of math problems for a gold star. After he has established consistent success with this arrangement, we can switch to having six lines earn one gold star.

Some of us may already have concerns.

GENERATION GAP?

No.

Agreed—we've increased the work requirement and kept the same level of pay.

However, this change in the work/pay situation is the *graduation* we discussed earlier.

We want the child to learn to do more and more and more and more work for each pay off.

This "trick of the trade" leads us to the next new topic.

57

Tricks of the trade

Weaning and leveling

Using this procedure, all we're doing is getting the kid *weaned* away from the reinforcers we've been using.

Experience shows that simply "leveling" with the kid is a useful thing to do at this time.

For example...

"Gertrude, I really don't think you need a gold star for every line of work you do anymore. You're doing *so* well. I'm very proud of you. Let's try two lines for a star from now on and see how that works."

If Gertrude is doing that well, she'll probably come around. You've discussed the situation with her, and she has been involved in making the *new contract*.

"But how about ME?"

If we are teachers, or if we have more than one child, we can predict what might happen . . .

"But Mom, he gets an extra TV show for brushing his teeth. I only get a 'Say, that's great Jake' once in a while, when I do it. That's not fair."

This situation can be handled, too. . .

"Jake, I know how you must feel, but Charlie is four years younger than you are. First of all, we let you stay out later at night on weekends. Also, you *really* don't need those things anymore. You've sort of *graduated* beyond that, don't you think?"

Recognize it?

That's **leveling.**

Chances are, Jake's going to recognize that Charlie needs that extra push (a *regular* reinforcer) to keep him going.

Plainly and simply stated, **appeal to Jake's better qualities,** and they'll show in a more obvious way.

Details

Kind of pay-off

Pay off with what kids like. We're silly if we always expect them to like what *we* value. (Really now, *one* short hemline doesn't make a girl into a streetwalker. Similarly, *one* lollipop doesn't rot away 20+ teeth).

Amount of pay-off

1. Don't be stingy.
2. Don't be too extravagant.

Pay off *just enough* to get the desired behavior.

If after a week or so, you don't get the results you expect, pay just a little more and see what happens. You may not yet have the child's attention.

Modeling

We've already highlighted how devastating punishment can be.

An additional drawback that punishment provides is that we (the adults) serve as models . . .

So, if I "blow my cool," when a kid disgusts me, I am providing him with a model for his behavior.

Instead of "blowing," . . .

1. withhold the wrath,
2. and in a calm voice,
3. say, "I didn't like that!"
4. Continue with, "Do *this . . . instead,* next time.

AND

Next time, *when he does it,* pay off.

You'll be shocked, as I was, at the favorable results.

When can I punish?

Punishment gets quick results, doesn't it?

Remember our earlier examples?

60

The only problem is that punishment doesn't have lasting results.

We generally use punishment *only* when we *must have* quick results, *now*.

Thus, it is fair to punish *only* . . .

1. when the child's own safety is endangered (running into the street), and
2. when someone else's safety is endangered (feeding Sister poison).

One last way—and use it *cautiously*—is "when learning is all fouled up."

For example...

Mrs. Jones (a speech teacher) is trying to help Mable to say *"thr"* in throw. Mable usually says *"frow."*

During the last session, Mable finally got it. She was doing beautifully.

Suddenly, during today's lesson Mable goes back to her old ways, and sometimes even ignores Mrs. Jones when she says, "Let's try it again, Mable."

Something *must* be done if further learning is to take place. We already have evidence that Mable can do it. She did it fine last week.

This is when we punish.

In a stern, clear voice Mrs. Jones says, "Mable, *stop it!* Listen to me and try. If you don't, I'll stop teaching you *early* today and you won't be able to earn enough points to buy free time when you go back to your class."

That should bring her around!

Remember though, use punishers *only* as last resorts.

When we use punishers too freely, we risk setting up *anxiety, escape,* and *avoidance reactions.*

An experiment 5

Increasing a
desirable behavior

Lovina is a "holy terror." For some unknown reason she runs to Teacher's desk all the time.

Things go like this:

"Lovina, here is your arithmetic. See these three rows of problems?"
"Uh-huh."

"You are to do all three rows. Do you understand?"
"Uh-huh."

"Now, remember, you'll get ten points for each row. If you do your work well, you'll have thirty points, and you can buy whatever you want from our CLASS MENU."

Teacher turns and starts toward her desk. Within seconds, Lovina is at Teacher's heels.

"Do you want me to do all three rows or just one Miss Florence?"

"How much time do I have left, Miss Florence?"

Again, *"Is this problem right, Miss Florence?"*

Once again, *"Could you show me how to do this one, Miss Florence?"*

And later, *"Why do I have to do this, Miss Florence?"*

Again, *"Miss Florence, do you know what I saw on TV last night?"*

And, *"Miss Florence, I gotta go potty."*

Then . . .

"Miss Florence, what was it I was supposed to do?"

Remarkable, isn't it! These things are common in so many classrooms.

What can Miss Florence do—short of murder?

Yes, she could blow her stack. Problem is, by early afternoon, Lovina would probably be back to her old tricks.

Let's get rid of it once and for all.

Usually, when we are working on a specific behavior, we try to keep some kind of records so we know where we've been and how much progress is being shown.

Louina

Let's use Lovina's behavior. She went to Miss
Florence's desk *without* permission eight times
in the dialogue above in about seventeen minutes.

Miss Florence wants to *reverse* this trend. She
wants Lovina to come to her desk *only when
Lovina has raised her hand*.

Notice, Miss Florence doesn't mind Lovina's *coming to the desk*—but permission or raising her hand is the issue.

Before Miss Florence starts trying to change Lovina's behavior, she has to find out about how frequently the no-no is *really* happening.

Beware at this point!

Because Miss Florence is ready to "blow her cool," the frequency probably SEEMS much greater than it really is. It's safer by far simply to keep a record of how frequently Lovina "goofs" each period for a few days.

It's more scientific too.

Then, Miss Florence has her evidence.

Gathering evidence

One way is to make a slash mark (/) or an X every time the "no-no" *occurs*. Another way is to make a mark every time a period goes by that the "no-no" doesn't occur.

The two cards below are samples of recording both ways.

MONDAY	MONDAY
X's show when the behavior OCCURS.	X's show when the behavior DOESN'T OCCUR.
Period	Period
1 XXXXX XXXXX XXXXX XXXX	1
2 XXXXX XXXXX XXXXX XX	2
*3	*3
4 XXXXX XXXXX XXXXX	4
5 XXXXX XXXXX XXXXX XXX	5
6 XXXXX XXXXX XXXXX X	6
7 XXXXX XXXXX XXXX	7
8 XXXXX XXXXX XXXXX X	8
*Lovina was in P.E.	*Lovina was in P.E.

Still another way to record it, and probably the best way would be to make marks every time the *desired* behavior (raising her hand) *occurs*.

Our record would look something like this. Obviously, none happened on the day shown above. Let's look at the record for the next day at school, Tuesday.

```
    TUESDAY
X's show HAND RAISING BEHAVIOR.
Period
    1 XX
    2 XXX
   *3
    4
    5 X
    6 XX
    7
    8 XX
*Lovina was in P.E.
Hand raises did not occur in
   periods 4 and 7.
```

Now the fun begins...

We are going to try to change Lovina's behavior. We want to increase or strengthen hand raising behavior.

We have already established that Lovina is reinforced by points that she can use to buy things from the class menu.

So, all we have to do is this . . .

"Lovina, starting tomorrow morning, you can earn two bonus points for each time you remember to raise your hand for help."

Now, under these *new* conditions . . .

67

Let's record what happens today.

```
WEDNESDAY
X's show HAND RAISES that got
REINFORCED.
  1 XXXXX XX
  2 XXXXX
 *3
  4 XXXX
  5 XXXXX X
  6
  7 XX
  8 XXXXX
*Lovina was in P.E.
```

Remember, Lovina may still be coming for help *without* raising her hand, but we're not recording *that*. Yep, you've got it. We're simply *ignoring* that behavior. Teacher just goes on with her work and poor Lovina stands and waits by Miss Florence's desk until it dawns on her "My gosh, I forgot to *raise my hand!*" Miss Florence doesn't have to say a thing.

Now, let's compare the last two cards, the *before* and *after*. The Tuesday card shows frequency without reinforcement.

TUESDAY	WEDNESDAY
WITHOUT POINTS	WITH POINTS
Period	Period
1. 2 hand raises	1. 7 hand raises
2. 3 hand raises	2. 5 hand raises
3. 0 hand raise	3. 0 hand raise
4. 0 hand raises	4. 4 hand raises
5. 1 hand raise	5. 6 hand raises
6. 2 hand raises	6. 0 hand raises
7. 0 hand raises	7. 2 hand raises
8. 2 hand raises	8. 5 hand raises
Total: 10 hand raises	Total: 29 hand raises

A helpful hint

You probably remember from earlier pages how we showed a change in one child's behavior— the fight scene.

You can do the same thing.

Line up your cards and shade over the X's like this.

No reinforcer   Reinforcing the desired Behavior

The cards show the frequency of a desired behavior (for three days).

Notice how simply we can see the progress.

In doing so, you have a continuous chart of progress.

Note:

For those classroom teachers who might be interested in trying to increase desirable behaviors in an entire class, the task is not really that forbidding. It can be done.

One way that has met with some success is this:

Simply place a small card on one corner of each child's desk. There's no need to tape them down.

Since teachers move up and down the rows spot checking a lot anyway, they can simply *add just one more step to that operation.* Assign a point value to *each part* of a child's assignment. Then, while walking around, if the work is being done *well,* award the points by writing a 5, a 10, or a 20 on his card. You won't even have to stop to explain or discuss it, because that takes up time unnecessarily. Simply award the points and keep on moving to other youngsters.

Later in the day, points can be cashed in for privileges or goodies that the kids want.

Another method that some teachers like is walking around handing out gold stars—with quite a lot of frequency. Stars equal 10 points and can later be traded for "stuff."

Finally, some teachers like to use small plastic disks. They simply walk around dropping "poker chip-like disks" into paper cups setting on the corner of each child's desk. Later, chips are traded for goodies.

In all these examples, you may be asking yourself. . .

1. But what if they tamper with the number of points I've written down on their cards?

   Simply state that anytime tampering is suspected or discovered, that child will lose *all* his points for that period or for that day.

   I'm certain that you recognize your writing well enough to know when someone's been tampering with it. Granted, some tampering will probably sneak by undetected. That's life. Never accept a "tattler's" word about another child. Cancel out points *only* when you can prove it yourself.

2. Or, what if they lose their card of stars, or some of the stars come unglued because of rough treatment? That's a tough break.

Teacher *only* pays off with purchasing power that can be supported *clearly* with gold stars. Next time, the youngster will take extra care to be certain that *no* stars are lost.

3. Maybe the chips will be traded among children. That's life. There are gamblers in real life. Let the sucker suffer the consequences. *Never* come to the rescue. Chances are, the sucker will never be taken in again.

4. And then there's the thief. Set up a stiff penalty for him when he is caught. But, if it's really easier to get chips, stars, or points simply by doing good work in class without an unreasonable amount of effort, there'll really be no need to steal.

(Turn to Appendix B. There's a complete set of sample procedures for implementing your own "Classroom Point System.")

Doing your own thing

6

This chapter will give some examples of children with problems. Before you try to help them solve their problems, follow these steps:

1. Decide what the problem is.

2. Ask yourself what you want to happen to the behavior.

>   Do you want it strengthened?
>   >   How do you strengthen behavior?
>   >   What will be your reinforcer?

>   Do you want it weakened?
>   >   How do you weaken behavior?
>   >   Will you use punishers or some other consequence?

3. Under what conditions do you want the desired behavior to occur or the undesirable behavior not to occur?

4. What will you use to reinforce the child?

5. How will you know when the behavior *occurs* or *doesn't occur?*

6. How are you going to prove your progress?

> You'll have to be able to prove how often it was occurring.

> You'll have to be able to prove how often it occurs now.

> Consider the use of slash marks, X's, recording the number of gold stars you hand out, the number of chips or points.

> In other words, you simply make a mark every time you deliver a reinforcer.

Now, let's get these kids shaped up!

Choose one –

Fritz has this problem—he still can't tie his shoes and he's nine. Help!

Jacob picks on other kids. Train him to stop.

Rhonda eats chalk. She probably won't die, but a twelve-year-old going around with chalk on her face looks pretty stupid. Help her.

Etta twists her hair. Can she be helped?

Emory bites his fingernails. We can't cut his fingers off. Help him.

Vernon won't keep busy in school. We can't get him a tutor. Help him. Better still, help his teacher solve the problem.

Irma works fast, but gets all the wrong answers. Straighten her out.

Gus cries when he doesn't get his way. Either muzzle him or change him!

Bud can read *some* words—a total of ten—and he's a third grader. Help.

Colette talks too loudly. What to do?

Colette talks too loudly

75

Myrtle butts in when others are talking. Help her to keep her friends.

Myrtle butts in

Jason is a thief. Cure him.

Mae exaggerates. Get her back on the right track.

Darrell hates school; he's stopped trying. Get him motivated.

Darrell hates school

Hazel "gets smart" with people. Stop her.

Lindsey won't wear his glasses; and he can't see.

Lindsey cant see

Marvin has a nervous twitch.

Annalou bites herself when she makes a poor grade in school.

Beulah whines and begs.

Annalou bites herself when she gets a poor grade

Beulah whines and bogs

Goodness knows each of these kids needs help. Help them. They're not crazy. They're not strange. They're really no different from any other "normal" child. See what you can do for them . . . who knows, one of your youngsters just might develop one of these behaviors someday. Should your world literally come to an end? I think not. Simply set out to solve the problem.

For practice, dream up some frequencies and mark off the behaviors. Write out the details of your experiment accounting for each of the steps listed in the beginning of this chapter. Use the sample experiment in the last chapter for additional help. If you forget the details of a technique that you're wanting to try, go back and read about it again.

Can I really do it?

We've been discussing how you teach in your classroom.

You do most of the things in this book already. That's why you love teaching. That's why you're a good teacher.

But, we've been developing some rather specific behavioral techniques and I'm sure you are asking—"Can I really use behavior modification?"

Of course you can, but let's put it in perspective.

Agreed, on the surface, behavior modification appears to be a reasonable and almost simple-minded method of child management—both for the school *and* home.

But, don't be fooled by this first impression. . .

Experience has shown that there's more to it than meets the eye.

There's a big difference between *any* two of the following:

1. understanding this manual,
2. being able to correctly describe these methods, and
3. really *doing* these things with your own students.

Consider, for example, that some coaches can tell us "how to become big stars," but they could never do it themselves.

Some people might say our coach hasn't "internalized" the very rules or tricks he's teaching his boys.

This may be true, I'm not sure.

However, to combat this problem—in other words, to graduate from the "talking about it stage" to the "doing it stage"—**we must practice it.**

If we think about it, we're going through the same processes that we plan to take the child through.

Rearranging our old methods into this new framework for child management requires *some* new learning for us adults, too.

The best possible way to see if you've got it, is to try it.

Start with one behavior—something small—and try to strengthen or weaken it.

Neither fantastic success nor remarkable failure will come immediately.

In fact, we'll probably mess up the first ten times we try to remember . . .

1. to reinforce that behavior or
2. to ignore this behavior.

The best description of the pain we'll go through is that it's at least as painful as . . .

Giving up Smoking
. . . or anything else you are accustomed to.

We are developing a new style using many of the same components from our old style.

Face it—most anything worth doing is difficult the first few times we try it.

The *reinforcer* for all our effort and pain comes with our *first success* . . .

at the end of three or four weeks of agony.

Some of the pitfalls we'll run across are:

1. When the desired behavior occurs, we weren't there to "catch him being good"—and we can't reinforce. It sneaked right by us.

2. When the desired behavior occurs, there's no proof or evidence. So, again we can't reinforce just 'cause Hazel says she tried.

If we do reinforce Hazel "simply for *saying* she tried" or "for *saying* she did it," then we're really not reinforcing properly. We're reinforcing talking about it. And, goodness knows, we all tell "little white lies" once in a while so someone will give us "just a little" reinforcer.

3. Or, we may be paying off like mad—praising Clyde everytime he uses his napkin—but, for some reason, Clyde doesn't seem to use the napkin more frequently.

Why?

Maybe **praise** doesn't turn **Clyde** on.

Some extra dessert might.

More pitfalls...

4. Then there's Elmer. He never puts away his boots. He's only three and you've been giving him a piece of candy every time he does it. But he never does it.

Maybe you're being a little "tightfisted." A whole candy bar instead might work. (15¢ or 20¢ a week for candy bars throughout the winter months won't destroy your grocery budget . . . or Elmer's teeth either.)

5. Or, perhaps Alfonso finally carries out the trash for us one night when he comes home from school.

DON'T:

"Alfonso, I'm going to tell your Dad how proud I am when he gets home. He'll have a nice surprise for you."

This is the *last* thing we might do, after we've been getting this behavior over a period of weeks.

DO:

"Alfonso, that's great! Have a nickel. You'll get one each time you remember to take out the trash after school."

Avoid delay.

Catch 'em being good and pay off. . .
IMMEDIATELY.

If Dad also wants to give a word of praise (or something else) later, that's fine, but it really won't have the impact of the *immediate* pay-off.

This same rule applies with baby sitters and anyone else who is with the child. Deliver the appropriate consequence *now,* when the behavior occurs. Don't wait until later and send a note home to Mommie. It's generally quite meaningless for Mommie either to praise or to spank or to ignore four hours later.

Catch 'em being good

An outline summary

7

Children behave and **behavior is learned.**

It is strengthened, weakened, or shaped by the behavior's consequences. Teachers may either (1) reward the behavior to increase its frequency of occurrence or (2) *not* reward the behavior to decrease its frequency of occurrence. Teachers may also punish behavior to decrease frequency, but undesirable side effects may be seen in the child's behavior.

I. Strengthening and Shaping Behavior

   A. Reinforcement should be **continuous.** When the behavior is more frequent, irregular reinforcement will "cement in" the behavior.

   B. Reinforcement should be **immediate.** Therefore, the child will see it as a consequence of his behavior.

   C. A reward must serve to **increase** the frequency of the desired behavior, or it is not a reinforcer.

   D. Rewards must be given in **sufficient** and **appropriate** quantity.

E. Rewards may be **extrinsic** or **intrinsic.**

    1. Extrinsic rewards are given the child by someone else (candy, toys, kisses, privileges, money, praise, hugs).

    2. Intrinsic rewards come from within the child in the form of interest for engaging in a certain behavior. The behavior supplies its own rewards (dresses self, does homework, gets good grades, brushes teeth).

F. Extrinsic rewards may be needed in the beginning to strengthen a desired behavior. After a while the behavior becomes rewarding in itself. Since we are all social beings, it is wise to offer some extrinsic rewards to supplement intrinsic rewards when teaching new skills.

G. Rewards should be offered for small steps in a "big" behavior (tying shoes) that you want to shape.

II. Weakening Behaviors

    A. Methods to weaken (decrease) behavior are:

        1. providing alternative behaviors

        2. reinforcing incompatible behaviors

        3. ignoring undesired behaviors

        4. punishment

    B. Alternative Behaviors
E.g.: "No, you may not play with the marbles, but you may wash the board."

    C. Incompatible Behaviors
E.g.: If you want a child not to walk around your classroom, say: "Sam, I am pleased that you are sitting in your seat as I asked,"—when he is.

D. Ignoring

Although for the child's protection, we cannot use this technique in all cases, it is a **highly effective method to eliminate behavior.**

E.g.: 1. Each time Sue calls out rather than raising her hand, ignore it.

2. Ignoring does not apply when Billy keeps running into the street.

E. Punishment (Harmful uses)

—most often used by adults, but is most **ineffective** because:

1. Punishment just represses undesired behavior. The behavior recurs despite the punishment, if it is mild.

2. Punishment creates harmful anxiety, escape, and avoidance which may be more harmful than the offense itself.

3. Physical punishment (spankings) provides children with adult models of aggression. (Thus, if parents get mad and hit, the child might think that he should be able to hit when he's mad.) **Children copy adult behavior.**

F. Punishment (Need for . . .)

—may be a useful training tool in **emergencies** only:

1. for quick training for safety,

2. when there is no way to reinforce an alternative or incompatible behavior and the undesired behavior **must stop** now . . . i.e., danger to self or to others.

G. Punishment (Acceptable Applications)

1. It must be given **immediately;**

2. It must be given with an explanation so the child can anticipate the same consequences in the future. (This situation occurs when you weren't able to warn the child that a new thing was a "no-no" before he was first introduced to it.)

3. It must be accompanied by the same set of words each time it is used. (E.g.: NO SMOKING; QUIET PLEASE, HOSPITAL ZONE)

Let's do this again sometime

Dear Colleague:

It's been an honor spending this brief time with you.

Indeed, modifying kids' behavior is difficult, fun, and challenging. No doubt most all of you already have success stories to tell. You simply would like more. Right?

The real utility of these techniques is shown best when we, as teachers, encounter that one youngster who we couldn't reach before. Now, we can!

Seriously try these techniques. In so doing, you'll be forced to scrutinize (1) yourself and (2) your student. Further, spot check yourself comparing your procedures with the suggestions in this little booklet. You'll by-pass some problems and avoid making errors.

Work, plan, and most of all—KEEP YOUR COOL.

Best personal regards,

Ron Carter

Appendix A
Survey quiz

PART I

1. Behavior is

_____ a. instinctive.   _____ b. motivated by drives.

_____ c. innate.   _____ d. learned.

2. If a desirable behavior increases in frequency, we can say that it is

_____ a. receiving no reinforcer.

_____ b. shaped.

_____ c. being reinforced.

_____ d. an example of shaping.

3. This manual is designed to give teachers

_____ a. an answer to all classroom management problems.

_____ b. a totally new way to communicate with children.

_____ c. a new system of management techniques.

_____ d. a completely new method for teaching the 3 R's.

4. This manual should be useful because

_____ a. teachers need specialized training in behavior management.

_____ b. teachers need a vocabulary for describing behavior more easily.

_____ c. they need to know principles of behavior which provide insight into children's motivation systems.

_____ d. behavior management is more important than skillful instruction in the tool subjects.

5. To get greater frequencies of a desirable behavior, one should first try

_____ a. teaching alternative behaviors.

_____ b. reinforcing that behavior.

_____ c. planned ignoring of all other behaviors.

_____ d. mild punishment for failure to show the desired behavior.

(1) D   (2) C   (3) C   (4) A   (5) B

6. Which three are methods of changing behavior?

_____ a. punishment, reinforcement, shaping
_____ b. strengthening, weakening, shaping
_____ c. ignoring, timing, avoidance
_____ d. escape, strengthening, reinforcement

7. Can teachers shape behavior?

_____ a. yes   _____ b. no

8. Alfonso is hitting his sister's doll house with his foot. Which method could probably weaken this behavior most effectively *with lasting effects?*

_____ a. a mild slap
_____ b. reporting the offense to "Mommie"
_____ c. ignoring the bad behavior and praising sister for no tantrum
_____ d. sister's crying loudly and for a long time

9. All behavior is controlled by

_____ a. M & M's.
_____ b. its impact on others.
_____ c. its benefit or lack of benefit to the behaver.
_____ d. authority figures.

10. In our "system" for behavior management, *reinforcement* means

_____ a. consequences that increase behavior.
_____ b. consequences that may or may not increase behavior.
_____ c. no consequences.
_____ d. shaping of behavior.

11. An effective reinforcer will *always*

_____ a. increase the frequency of a behavior.
_____ b. reduce deviant behavior.
_____ c. be reinforcing to all children.
_____ d. decrease the frequency of a behavior.

12. To increase the frequency of the desired behavior, the consequence (reinforcer) must be

_____ a. food.
_____ b. given by the classmates.
_____ c. given by the teacher.
_____ d. immediate.

(6) B   (7) A   (8) C   (9) C   (10) A   (11) A   (12) D

13. A quick, easy, practical, and reliable way to record frequency of behavior as it occurs is

_____ a. making marks on a pad.

_____ b. hiring an "observer."

_____ c. keeping a mental count.

_____ d. purchasing a special recorder.

14. *Specifying* the desired behavior is a rule for strengthening behavior. However, it is unnecessary because

_____ a. children are brighter than we think.

_____ b. regardless—the behavior that is reinforced will be the one that is increased.

_____ c. teachers need to make sure the behavior they want to recur is the one they are reinforcing.

_____ d. children really don't need insight into their own behavior.

15. When is it best to *specify* the desired behavior or to give *hints?*

_____ a. under the proper conditions for the desired behavior to occur

_____ b. as the desirable behavior occurs

_____ c. as the children are shaped up

_____ d. as the punisher occurs

16. "Don't ignore" refers to

_____ a. punishment and violation of rules.

_____ b. occurrence of desirable behaviors.

_____ c. needs of the children.

_____ d. children, in general.

17. Shaping is a method for

_____ a. teaching complex behavior by progressive steps.

_____ b. weaning children from reinforcers.

_____ c. decreasing an undesirable behavior.

_____ d. arranging the physical environment of the classroom.

18. *Who* determines what is reinforcing?

_____ a. the teacher

_____ b. the classroom environment

_____ c. the child

_____ d. immediacy of the reinforcement

(13) A   (14) B   (15) A   (16) B   (17) A   (18) C

19. If a child gets too much reinforcement for desired behavior,

_____ a. teachers and parents may have to resort to punishment to control his misbehaviors.

_____ b. the frequency of the behavior may not be affected
at all.

20. Using the wrong things as a reinforcer will lead to

_____ a. a decrease in the desired behavior.

_____ b. an increase in the desired behavior.

_____ c. no change in the desired behavior.

_____ d. wrongly shaped behavior.

_____ e. no change *or* a decrease in the desired behavior.

21. Too little reward will lead to

_____ a. no change in behavior.

_____ b. an increase in the desired behavior.

_____ c. a decrease in the desired behavior.

_____ d. incorrectly weakened behavior.

22. In teaching a behavior, irregular reinforcement should be used
only

_____ a. immediately.

_____ b. after the behavior is taught.

_____ c. on very young children.

_____ d. to initially "cement in" the behavior.

23. The purpose of keeping records during an experiment in modifying behavior is to

_____ a. be able to compare before and after frequencies of
the behavior.

_____ b. show the child that you planned to modify his
behavior.

_____ c. show what reinforcers serve to modify the child's
behavior.

_____ d. determine the amount of reinforcer to be used.

24. Avoidance is

_____ a. a reaction to punishment.

_____ b. a neutral event.

_____ c. a reinforcer.

_____ d. a punisher.

(19) B   (20) E   (21) A   (22) B   (23) A   (24) A

25. A slap is usually a (n)
    _____ a. reinforcer.
    _____ b. punisher.
    _____ c. substitute behavior.
    _____ d. immediate consequence for a desired behavior.

26. Severe punishment
    _____ a. avoids the need for reinforcing another behavior.
    _____ b. does not teach desirable behaviors.
    _____ c. has temporary side effects such as escape and avoidance.
    _____ d. never loses its effectiveness.

27. A danger of using physical punishment (spankings) is that
    _____ a. it is immoral and wrong.
    _____ b. it reinforces crying behavior.
    _____ c. it provides an adult model for hitting behavior.
    _____ d. it decreases the frequency of the undesirable behavior.

28. A teacher or parent who is a poor source of reward is probably best described as a persistent
    _____ a. reinforcer.
    _____ b. model.
    _____ c. shaper.
    _____ d. punisher.

29. Carol is two and is playing with poison. You should
    _____ a. reinforce a substitute behavior.
    _____ b. punish *that* behavior.
    _____ c. ignore *that* behavior so it will weaken.
    _____ d. reason with Carol about the dangers of poison.

30. Providing a substitute behavior is a method for
    _____ a. decreasing the frequency of an undesirable behavior.
    _____ b. punishing undesirable behavior.
    _____ c. increasing motivation.
    _____ d. ignoring desirable behavior.

(25) B   (26) B   (27) C   (28) D   (29) B   (30) A

31. Punishment should be administered _____ to be effective.

_____ a. occasionally
_____ b. regularly
_____ c. in anticipation of the offense
_____ d. immediately

32. If you come when I call you, I should _____ your behavior.

_____ a. shape
_____ b. reinforce
_____ c. punish
_____ d. model

33. Teaching a substitute behavior is a method for

_____ a. indirectly punishing a child.
_____ b. increasing an undesirable behavior.
_____ c. decreasing an undesirable behavior.
_____ d. weakening a desirable behavior.

34. Ignoring a behavior will cause that behavior to

_____ a. increase.
_____ b. decrease.
_____ c. remain stable.
_____ d. vary indefinitely.

(31) D   (32) B   (33) C   (34) B

PART II

Where space is not given for your answer, please use a separate sheet.

1. Two directions to change behavior are to

   _____   _____

2. Consequences for behavior can be either one of the three following:

   _____ _____ _____

3. How can a consequence for a given behavior be neutral?

4. Withholding a reinforcer should result in

   _____

5. What should be done to weaken the frequency of a behavior?

6. When could it occur that a reward given by the teacher fails to increase the frequency of the desired behavior? Give two instances.

7. A reinforcer *always* _____

   _____

8. Some teachers' rewards are not _____ because they do not increase the frequency of the desired behavior.

9. If you delay a reinforcer, what would probably happen?

10. Occasional reinforcement of the desired behavior is called

    _____.

11. Never ignore the occurrence of a _____ behavior.

12. All behavior is _____.

13. Based on the ideas in this manual, it would seem that the failure of a child to learn would be totally the fault of the _____ environment   _____ child   _____ teacher

14. Teaching—good teaching, that is—involves providing *hints* for _____ behavior so that the child knows what is expected.

ANSWERS ON NEXT PAGE.

ANSWERS

1. strengthen   weaken

2. reinforcers, punishers, neutral (blah) events

3. A consequence can be neutral if it fails to either increase or to decrease the desired behavior. (Example: Smiles and pats on the head may not be reinforcing to some disadvantaged youngsters.)

4. a decrease in the behavior being changed.

5. a. ignore that behavior, or
   b. provide an alternative (substitute) for that behavior, or
   c. teach an incompatible behavior, or
   d. withhold reinforcement, or
   e. punish the behavior *in an emergency only.*

6. a. The reward may not be reinforcing to that child.
   b. The child is already "filled up" on that reward.

7. increases the frequency of a behavior.

8. reinforcing

9. There would probably be little change in the target behavior because reinforcement must be immediate.

10. irregular or intermittent reinforcement. It "cements in" behavior.

11. desired or desirable

12. learned or taught.

13. teacher

14. target or desired

15. Ignoring the occurrence of a desired behavior at the early stages of training may lead to a _____ in learning the desired behavior.

16. What kind of skill or task are we teaching when we decide to use shaping?

17. Cite an example of a skill or task which could be taught by the use of shaping.

18. Why is shaping valuable?

19. Explain what a reinforcer should do for a behavior you are trying to teach a child.

20. How much reinforcement should be used? Why is this issue important?

21. What are the possible consequences of giving too little reward?

22. It is wise to try to reinforce a new behavior _____ it occurs.

23. When is irregular reinforcement advisable?

24. What is the value of making marks or X's on a card when you are trying to modify or change a child's behavior? List several reasons.

25. What is the value of having *two* phases in a program to change a behavior?

26. What might you do if you have started reinforcing Brenden with pats on the head for remaining seated instead of running around the room . . . and the "running around the room behavior" fails to decrease? List more than one solution.

27. Punishment, when used by teachers and parents, is usually intended to _____ an undesired behavior.

28. _____ govern our behavior by determining whether it will or will not increase in frequency.

ANSWERS ON NEXT PAGE.

ANSWERS

15. failure or decrease

16. a complex skill or one with many steps, such as long division, adding columns, or tying one's shoes.

17. See Answer 16.

18. Shaping allows the parent or teacher to teach COMPLEX behaviors by building together the teaching of several small skills which are all related to or a part of the complex skill.

19. The reinforcer should increase the frequency of the target behavior.

20. A sufficient amount to maintain the target behavior.

Some children can get satiated or "filled up" on a reinforcer; thus, the result is no change in behavior beyond that point. OR, some children require large amounts of a given reinforcer to change their behavior.

21. The target behavior may show no change.

22. every time

23. It is advisable during the later phase of training. After you have obtained an increase in the frequency of the desired behavior, you may elect to switch from REGULAR to IRREGULAR reinforcement in an effort to "cement in" the desired behavior.

24. (a) Teachers can make comparisons between Phase I and Phase II and determine the success or lack of success of the behavior change program for both the *before* and the *after* phases.
    (b) Teachers can show the child how his behavior is changing.
    (c) Teachers can demonstrate to parents the amount of change in the behavior of their child.
    (d) There is less stress and strain for both teachers, parents, and children when a system for behavior management is used in the classroom. Expectations are *clearer*.
    (e) Teachers are not forced to rely on their memories or their own judgment as to whether the child is actually showing improvement. They have the data in black and white.
    (f) There is less of a tendency to question reports written on the basis of objective information of this sort than there is to question impressionistic teacher reports.

(g) These systems deal only with *observable* behaviors; therefore, the teachers and parents are not forced to speculate about what factors might be motivating the child's behavior such as aggressive tendencies toward authority figures, etc.

(h) Teachers, by virtue of their systematic use of this framework, will be in a better position to make *realistic* statements about how to get a child to show a specific change in his behavior—this could be helpful to other teachers as well as parents.

25. These two phases are needed for the purposes of comparison. One needs to determine the frequency of the target behavior *before* and *after* the "treatment," so he can make a judgmental statement about the degree of success or failure of the "treatment."

26. Check to see if
    a. another reinforcer would be more effective.
    b. your reinforcer is immediate.
    c. you are reinforcing every instance of the desired behavior.
    d. you are giving too much reinforcer.
    e. you are giving too little reinforcer.
    f. some other powerful reinforcer is maintaining the undesirable behavior—which washes out the effect of your reinforcer.

27. weaken or eliminate

28. Consequences (punishers or reinforcers)

29. Spankings are a form of _____.

30. Getting hit by a car is a _____ for running into the street.

31. The one biggest criticism of the use of punishment is that it fails to teach _____
_____.

32. Can you say definitely that punishment will always reduce the frequency of an undesirable behavior? Discuss.

33. A reduction in the frequency of a given behavior implies that any one of several conditions may be present. List some of the possible conditions.

34. Escape is a(n) _____.

35. Truancy from school is a form of _____.

36. Running away from school is a form of _____
_____.

37. Anxiety is a reaction to _____.

38. To weaken an undesired behavior, it must be followed by consequences which _____ that behavior in frequency.

39. Extremely severe punishment will probably cause
_____
_____

40. Ridicule is a punishment intended by its users to _____ the _____ of an undesirable behavior.

41. A drawback associated with the use of spankings and the like by teachers and parents is that it provides the child with a _____ for such behavior.

42. The control of a child's behavior through the use of nagging will usually _____ with continued use.

43. Is there a time when it is necessary to punish the child? When?

44. Like reinforcement, punishment must be delivered _____ to be effective.

ANSWERS ON NEXT PAGE.

ANSWERS

29. punishment

30. consequence or punishment

31. the desired behavior or the alternative for the punished behavior.

32. No. Some children seem to thrive on rebukes from adults. That's the only way that they can get the attention they want.

    Further, remember that what may be a punisher for you may not be for someone else. In fact, it may be a reinforcer for him.

33. a. Punishment may have occurred.
    b. Someone may be teaching an incompatible behavior.
    c. Someone may be teaching an alternative behavior.
    d. There may be no real reinforcer maintaining the behavior, so it drops out.
    e. There may be too much reinforcement for a given period of time, so you need to switch reinforcers.
    f. There may be too little reinforcement to sustain the behavior—at least for that child.
    g. You may be using the wrong reinforcer (Same as d).

34. reaction to punishment.

35. avoidance.

36. escape.

37. punishment.

38. decrease

39. anxiety reactions, escape reactions, avoidance reactions, or a decrease in the target behavior.

40. decrease   frequency

41. model

42. decrease

43. YES.
    a. when training must be rapid for reasons of safety
    b. when reinforcement is ineffective
    c. when reinforcement is bothersome (not much time)

44. immediately

45. Is providing a substitute behavior a method for strengthening or weakening behavior? Explain.

46. What is the purpose for associating special words with punishment when punishment is necessary?

ANSWERS

45. It is generally associated with weakening.

The heart of the issue is that you are either not completely pleased or simply displeased with a current behavior the child is showing. One way to lessen the problem is to provide him with a substitute behavior for those situations.

46. You are using a combination or a two-part consequence here. You are punishing and using a set of signal words (hints) simultaneously. Hopefully, in the not too distant future, you will be able to drop out the actual punisher and use only the punishing words.

Appendix B
A classroom point system

The Classroom Situation

A teacher recently advised her supervisor that several problem behaviors in her classroom were interfering with academic/social performance. She requested assistance with management of these problems, hoping to increase the probability of re-entry of her students to regular classroom instruction. Very receptive to suggestions, she was willing and eager to implement any reasonable procedures designed to increase constructive control and/or productiveness in her classroom. She listed several deviant behaviors needing to be reduced. These behaviors are listed below:

1. teasing (name-calling)
2. abusive language (unkind comments)
3. daydreaming (off-task)
4. refusal to work
5. asking to be placed back into regular classes*
6. calling the class an EMH or dumb class
7. pestering neighbors
8. talking without raising hand
9. only partial completion of assignments
10. chronic griping
11. hitting classmates
12. out-of-seat behavior

*Of course, this is not an entirely undesirable goal.

Suggested Procedures

1. The teacher peruses training manual on behavior modification.

2. The teacher generates a list of "Ways to Earn $" (more commonly known as class rules). Each of the rules, individually, or in composite will be listed in a POSITIVE fashion, e.g.,

   a. keeping hands to oneself
   b. working quietly
   c. asking for help, rather than griping when things go wrong
   d. raising hand to talk, etc.

In addition, some behaviors that are incompatible with deviant

103

performance will also be added to the "Ways to Earn $."

    e. completing assignments
    f. talking quietly during free time
    g. walking quietly in the hall
    h. leaving room quietly
    i. returning to room quietly,
      etc.

3. The teacher, in collaboration with the class, generates a "Class Menu," i.e., a list of those things that the students want to work for in her class—*not* what she thinks they should want. Appendix C lists typical items (pay-offs) of a class menu.

4. By hand vote, the class as a whole helps the teacher to rank the privileges, activities, and/or items in their order of desirability.

5. The teacher arbitrarily assigns point values to the items on the menu.

6. The teacher advises that beginning NOW, students will be rewarded for their doing "good things" in class.

7. As students engage in the desired behaviors listed above (non-occurrence of griping, daydreaming, etc.) they are rewarded IMMEDIATELY. As classroom behavior comes under better control, the teacher can delay delivery of earnings to the end of *each* class period; later she can delay to the end of a.m. and p.m. sessions.

8. For all "seat work" (written) assignments, a contractual agreement is made with each student on an individual basis. As assignments (contracts) are fulfilled, papers are turned in, graded, and students will be:

    a. paid for completion and
    b. paid bonus points for correct answers.

A copy of a contract follows.

104

CONTRACT	CONTRACT	
Teacher's Stub		date
	I, _____	
	understand that I will receive $_____ for	
Name	this assignment _____,	
	and _____ as a bonus, if completed by	
Date	_____.	
Amount	student's initials	teacher's initials

9. Payment is made with various denominations of play money. It is helpful to print each denomination on a different color.

   Judgments regarding "how much it's worth" are based on the teacher's evaluation of:

   a. how much the student can do and
   b. how hard it is for him.

   Obviously, if pay remains the same (approximately) while difficulty level is gradually increasing, the child will be slowly weaned away from his need for rewards to sustain his performance, i.e., he will be working much more, while continuing to receive much less.

   When a student is consistently performing at a fairly high level, but still is not up to his grade level, the amount of "pay-off" can *also* be reduced, so even *more* work must be done to obtain the same amount of reward—at day's end.

   Students will be forced to *really* "get on the stick."

10. Money is made useful by giving it "purchasing power" for special privileges and activities that students may buy.

    In general, there should be a "store time" near the end of the school day so students can buy this free time for games, listening to the radio, drawing, washing boards, etc. However, students should also be allowed (when they're having an especially bad day) to buy some "loafing time," even during regular class time. Such a practice will obviously be doubly costly, since

a. they must pay to loaf and
b. they won't be earning points for good work during that time.

11. I.O.U.: At day's end, should students fail to spend all their money and prefer to save up, the teacher may issue an I.O.U. that may be exchanged later for activities. An I.O.U. is shown below.

I.O.U.	I.O.U.
Teacher's Stub	_____ date
_____ Name	I, _____ (name of student)
_____ Date	have $_____ in savings to be added to tomorrow's earnings.
_____ Amount	_____ _____ student's initials teacher's initials

12. Savings: To encourage savings (ability to *delay* reward) which is an approximation of more adult behavior, the teacher may allow the "richer" students to bid for a "Super Surprise" on Fridays. She plans to bake a weekly or monthly cake, batch of cookies, etc. (Local administrative morale and fiscal support would be advisable in this connection.)

Needless to say, these "super surprises" will be *very* costly and tempting. But . . . .

13. An even more desirable reward (even more delayed) would possibly be gaining re-entry into regular classes once more.

The following conditions could be imposed:

a. Academic achievement within one year of the student's "expected" grade level
b. General performance of 90% accuracy or above
c. No violations of social behavior for one month
d. $50,000 (in play money)

All these lead to right to re-enter any *one* class of the student's choice.

Successful (sustained) performance for two weeks or more

106

in *that one class* plus \$25,000, earns purchase of a second class in regular grades and so on.

These arrangements (contracts) should be clearly specified and agreed to by the student, teachers, and administrative personnel. Failure to fulfill the provisions of an agreement (in real life) is regarded as a breach of contract (generation gap) and is subject to legal action (student militants).

Therefore, realistic and feasible contracts should be adhered to. They can be renegotiated with the consent and approval of all interested parties.

14. In the case of uncooperative behavior of *any* student (refusal to work, talking during a movie), it should be announced that:

"_____, you have lost your earning power during this movie for talking and disturbing others."

Persistent failure to comply should include placement (with no work to do) of the student in the corridor for a brief, but designated, period of time. When time is up say,

"You can earn \$_____ by going to your seat quietly and \$_____ by starting your _____.
                                                       assignment

The student obviously loses earning power while isolated in the corridor.

Further violation of the same sort should include a trip to the administrator's office. The student should be directed to a "pre-planned" seat and given *absolutely no attention* from secretaries, building administrator, or guidance personnel. It should be prearranged that trips to the office will be accompanied by an intercom call from the teacher saying,

"_____ is on his way to the office. He is to stay there for _____ minutes. Please be sure he returns at _____ a.m./p.m."

Upon the student's return, the teacher should again say,

"_____ is back and is ready to work. Thank you for helping him and me."

ALL school personnel should be *strongly* dissuaded from engaging in dialogue such as:

"Are you in trouble again?"
"What have you done now?"
"Why are you here?"
"Come into my office and let's talk about it."
"Could you come to my office later to talk about this?"

For the teacher to sustain complete control of her students' behavior (academic/social) she must have the cooperation of and *lack of* interference from all other school personnel.

In all cases, it would be obvious to all who "need" to know that _____ *is* in trouble again. Pursuing the issue via dialogue will simply serve to reward or attend to the student's engaging in deviant behavior. The teacher and the student will simply have to rework their earlier gains if such inadvertent sabotage occurs.

This procedure is referred to technically as "time out from positive reward." The student is simply removed from the conditions under which he may earn "money" because his performance was not "on-task." It is a slower but a more permanent means of decreasing the frequency of undesirable behaviors. Punishment, similarly, will reduce the frequency— even faster—but results are not sustained. Rather the behavior *will* ironically escalate and return to the same or a higher frequency (based on experimental evidence). Finally, punishers have other undesirable side effects:

a. The punisher causes "aversive" actions (escape and/or avoidance).
b. The student may show anxiety (frustration) or aggressive behavior in subsequent confrontations.

Conclusion

There is no doubt that implementation of this program will be extremely difficult for the teacher. It will require sustained support of administrative personnel and a long-term willingness to "give it a try" for a minimum of six weeks.

In brief, one may quickly assume:

1. that these relatively global recommendations will completely inhibit teacher style, and
2. that student behavior (if our goals are readily met) will be too

108

rigidly confined to doing only what they're paid to do.

This conclusion can readily be supported, if these expectations are held for the program. Indeed, the results will become a self-fulfilling prophecy.

On the other hand, the foregoing recommendations can be used merely as they are intended—as a means for re-establishing consistent and predictable control over *relevant* (to future, adult success) pupil behaviors. As they show competence in meeting the criteria set for their individual performances, it is clearly the teacher's responsibility to renegotiate goals at the next higher level of performance desired. In so doing, students will be

1. weaned away from this rather concrete token economy, and
2. *gradually* trained to sustain performance for "social reinforcers" (praise or recognition).

To accomplish the latter on a regular basis will undoubtedly be a new set of behaviors for most of these students. Their performance will be shaky and tenuous at times but can be established firmly with practice. Since they don't currently function like the "garden-variety junior high student" (regardless of their chronological ages), it must be assumed that "good school work" and "good social interaction" are new behavioral clusters that must be clearly, discreetly, and deliberately taught.

A teacher's eagerness and willingness to "tackle" the tasks at hand are clear indications that success is just around the corner—maybe a mile down the path, but just around the corner! No aspect of teaching can be totally insurmountable; difficult—yes, but soluble!

Appendix C
Some pay-offs for school-aged kids

Elementary grades

Lead flag salute

Choose seat for specified time

Choose book to review for class

Select topic for group to discuss

Read to a friend

Read with a friend

Right to tutor a slower classmate

Free time in the library

Be in a class play

Help teacher hand out papers, go to office, erase board, empty trash, dust off desks, sharpen pencils

Work at chalkboard

5 minutes to discuss something with teacher

Ask child what he would like to do

Plan a class trip

Plan a class project

Time to read aloud

Perform small duties

Select game or object for recess

Work puzzle (free time)

Draw, paint, work with clay, etc.

Choose group activity

Take a "good" note home to mom (arrange a reward with the mother)

Extend class recess by specified number of minutes

Play teacher

10 minute break to choose game and play with a friend, QUIETLY

Class party

Use language master

Listen to record with earphones

See a filmstrip

Bring something special to show the class

Use radio with earphones

Have a "fun" movie

Dance in the gym

Use tape recorder

Work puzzle

Draw a picture

Paint with tempera

Build with construction blocks

Model with play dough

Candy

Dry cereal

Comic book

Chocolate instead of white milk

Extra carton of milk

A cookie along with the milk

Accumulate points for purchasing doll clothes (funny money)

Marbles

Pencil

Eraser

"Hot Wheel" cars

Compliment

Smile approval

Secondary grades

Extra time for doing homework in class

Extra time in gym, home ec room, shop, music room, etc.

Right to work independently on a special project for another class

Work in school office

Work in guidance office

Work in school library

Open discussion of social issues

Right to work as a tutor for elementary youngsters

Time to paint scenery for class play

Time for looking at own magazines

Class party

Have a "fun" movie (e.g. W. C. Fields)

Dismiss period early

Dismiss school early

Plan a special school function

Extra time for committees to meet

Time for club meetings

Dance in the gym

Time to practice something

Time to pursue a hobby at school

111

Time to interview local merchants for a class project

Right to sign up for or to "audit" some extra class(es)

Help teacher by making a visual aid for teacher to use with another group of students

Display good work

Pull the drapes for film showing

Carry a message to the office

Use of radio with earphones

Free time in student lounge

A class Coke break

Name in the newspaper for special achievements other than grades

Work on school yearbook or newspaper

Write special article for school news

Plan a class trip

Released time to work as a "candy striper" at local hospital

Released time to go to gym and shoot baskets